Guess Who
Roars

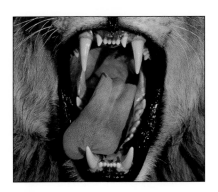

Sharon Gordon

BENCHMARK BOOKS

MARSHALL CAVENDISH
NEW YORK

Can you see me in the tall grass?

I am a very large cat.

I weigh about 400 pounds.

I live in Africa.

My family is called
a *pride*.

Our babies are
called cubs.

They stay safe in
our *den*.

I hunt at night.

I eat zebras and other animals.

I can run fast.

I can move very quietly.

I can even climb a tree.

I see well with my eyes.

My hearing is even better.

I am strong.

I have powerful paws.

I have sharp claws.

16

Look at my long teeth.

They help me rip my food into pieces.

I rest in the sunshine after eating.

I sleep up to 20 hours a day!

I have thick gold hair called a *mane*.

It is hard to see me in the dry grass.

But you can hear me!

My roar is like thunder.

Who am I?

I am a lion!

Who am I?

eye

mane

paws

roar

teeth

Challenge Words

den
A lion's home.

mane
Thick hair that grows on a lion's head or neck.

pride
A family of lions.

29

Index

Page numbers in **boldface** are illustrations.

About the Author

Sharon Gordon has written many books for young children. She has also worked as an editor. Sharon and her husband Bruce have three children, Douglas, Katie, and Laura, and one spoiled pooch, Samantha. They live in Midland Park, New Jersey.

With thanks to Nanci Vargus, Ed.D. and
Beth Walker Gambro, reading consultants

Benchmark Books
Marshall Cavendish
99 White Plains Road
Tarrytown, New York 10591-9001
www.marshallcavendish.com

Library of Congress Cataloging-in-Publication Data

Gordon, Sharon.
Guess who roars / by Sharon Gordon.
p. cm. — (Bookworms: Guess who)
Includes index.
Summary: Clues about the lion's physical characteristics, behavior, and
habitat lead the reader to guess what animal is being described.
ISBN 0-7614-1556-4
1. Lions—Juvenile literature. [1. Lions.] I. Title. II. Series:
Gordon, Sharon. Bookworms: Guess who.

QL737.C23G65 2003
599.757—dc21
2003001118

Photo Research by Anne Burns Images

Cover Photo by: *Visuals Unlimited*/Barbara Gerlach

The photographs in this book are used with permission and through the courtesy of: *Animals Animals:*
pp. 1, 19, 29 (right) H. Pooley; p. 13 Animals Animals; p. 21 Len Rue; p. 23 Hamman/Heldring;
p. 27 Alfred B. Thomas. *Peter Arnold*: p. 3 BIOS (Seitre); p. 9 Gunter Ziesler; pp. 17, 28 (lower) Gerard Lacz;
pp. 25, 29 (left) BIOS (M & C Denis-Huot). *Visuals Unlimited*: pp. 5, 28 (top right) Barbara Gerlach;
p. 7 Will Trayer; p. 11 1992 G.L.E.; pp. 15, 28 (top left) Ksell B. Sandved.

Series design by Becky Terhune

Printed in China
1 3 5 6 4 2